BRITAIN'S ⚏ HERITAGE

Road Rollers

Anthony Coulls

AMBERLEY

Acknowledgements

I would like to thank Ian Cooper for the front cover image, of Aveling & Porter Convertible steam roller *Lady Hesketh* taken at a steam party in North Shropshire. Other images were taken by the author or Peter Coulls or are from the collections of Anthony Coulls, Peter Coulls and Hedd Jones. Thanks too in particular are due to Peter Galliford for his reminiscences and permission to use photos from his collection and also David Mitchell for some of the colour images of working engines, taken by him or his late brother Robert. Peter Coulls and Hedd Jones proofread the text and made helpful suggestions for content.

This book is dedicated to all the friends I have made over a lifetime of road rolling enthusiasm, in particular Trevor Daw, the Milns Family, Derek Rayner and my colleagues, the South of Durham Engine Men. I also dedicate it to my wife Kathryn, who had never been near a road roller when we first met, and who has been incredibly supportive of my fascination over the years.

First published 2018

Amberley Publishing
The Hill, Stroud
Gloucestershire, GL5 4EP

www.amberley-books.com

Copyright © Anthony Coulls, 2018

The right of Anthony Coulls to be identified as the Author of this work has been asserted in accordance with the Copyrights, Designs and Patents Act 1988.

ISBN 978 1 4456 7580 0 (paperback)
ISBN 978 1 4456 7581 7 (ebook)

All rights reserved. No part of this book may be reprinted or reproduced or utilised in any form or by any electronic, mechanical or other means, now known or hereafter invented, including photocopying and recording, or in any information storage or retrieval system, without the permission in writing from the Publishers.

British Library Cataloguing in Publication Data.
A catalogue record for this book is available from the British Library.

Printed in the UK.

Contents

1
Introduction

The need to improve the UK road system saw a number of developments in the nineteenth century. To allow people to travel more safely and faster, smoother roads were needed and the tools to make them so. The road roller began as a horse-drawn device, followed by the favourite, the steam roller, seen on British roads for over a century. As technology changed, the rollers began to get lighter and new ways of propulsion – petrol and diesel – came in and while these continue to this day, the term 'steam roller' has entered popular culture, even though motor roller is what the machine will often be these days. The basic function of a deadweight compacting device remains, but the appeal of the steam roller is far greater – and hundreds survive to this day with enthusiasts. Even diesel and petrol rollers now have their following as they are a very accessible way into the vintage restoration world. This book looks at the past and present of road rollers and the ephemera surrounding the road making scene.

To look at the need for road rollers, we need to examine the way that the roads were built in the period leading up to the introduction of rollers. While there have been roads in the United Kingdom from the Roman period, the science and practice of making roads and the consequent history are long and complex, along with the full development of the road system. The need for rolling a road really resulted from the adoption of John Loudon McAdam's (1756–1836) design of a good, cambered, weatherproof road surface. This was achieved by compacting a 30 cm layer of graded small stones on the subsoil and consolidating them by pressure. Traffic and use provided the main source of further consolidation, resulting in a road that could withstand a fair amount of wear without being cut up into ruts as previous roads were prone to. In this way the roads that carried the Industrial Revolution traffic were developed, though the network itself dated back centuries.

Contemporary with McAdam was Thomas Telford. In 1801 Telford worked for the British Commission of Highlands Roads and Bridges, and became director of the Holyhead Road Commission between 1815 and 1830. Telford used roughly 30 cm × 25 cm × 15 cm partially shaped paving stones (pitchers), with a slight flat face on the bottom surface. He turned the other faces vertically. The longest edge was arranged crossways to the traffic direction, and the joints were broken in the method of conventional brickwork, but with the smallest faces of the pitcher forming the upper and lower surfaces.

Broken stone was wedged into the spaces between the tapered perpendicular faces to provide the layer with good lateral control. Telford kept the natural formation level and used masons to camber the upper surface of the blocks. He placed a 15 cm layer of stone no bigger than 6 cm on top of the rock foundation. To finish the road surface, he covered the stones with a mixture of gravel and broken stone. This structure came to be known as 'Telford pitching'. Telford's road depended on a resistant structure to prevent water from collecting and corroding the strength of the pavement. Telford raised the pavement structure above ground level whenever possible.

Road rollers began as horse-drawn implements; here's one on the Bilton Road in Rugby at an unknown date to give an impression of the scale of the operation, not a great size or weight.

Telford's method needed a heavy roller to roll the smaller stone into the pitchers and consolidate the pitchers into the formation. (This is why lots of heavy rollers were made in the early period of steam rolling). This method was widespread as recently as after the Second World War as it needed less construction depth than McAdam's method to get a stiff and durable surface. Even today, my brother-in-law will often dig up a 'Telford' road in Shropshire which is no more than 12 inches deep, the top 2 or 3 inches being successive layers of tar and chip.

In towns, the dramatic increase in traffic was countered by street widening, the road surface itself being either macadam, cobblestones, stone setts or wooden blocks covered by tar – the latter wore away rapidly and then created a slipping hazard. The only aid to construction was the use of mobile horse-drawn coal-fired tar boilers on site to melt tar, which was then poured around stone setts. The surface of macadam roads and streets was levelled by the use of hand or horse-drawn rollers, sometimes borrowed from agricultural applications where grassland or fields needed rolling. The weight of such rollers – and thus their effectiveness – was limited, otherwise they would become uncontrollable on hills. Some form of mechanical or powered intervention was necessary as the road network grew and traffic of all sorts increased.

The Beginnings

In 1865, the first steam roller made its appearance in Britain, a long-lasting invention which transformed road works. The steam-powered road roller was to survive at work for over a century in a number of locations and entered the era of motorways – a really long period for a piece of plant. The diesel and petrol road rollers appeared some forty years later, and remain in use to the current time.

Did you know?

The first steam roller was made in France; unusual when one considers that the steam locomotive and traction engine were British inventions. Dating from 1860, it would be five years before the steam roller found its way to Britain as the original French machines, at 30 tons, were too heavy for British applications.

The steam roller followed on from the steam traction engine – a self-propelled steam engine which grew out of the portable engines made for agriculture. Thomas Aveling, a Kent farmer, said it was a shame to see a steam engine drawn by six horses rather than being able to use its own power to drive itself along. Aveling took a Clayton & Shuttleworth portable engine in 1859 and made it self-moving with a chain drive to the wheels. A horse in shafts still provided the steering at the front, but it wasn't long before mechanical means, with either a ship's wheel or tiller, were tried. Developments and alterations came thick and fast, with gear drive and worm and gear steering being two major steps forward. The classic shape of the traction engine began to emerge by the late 1860s and the adaption to other applications including a steam-powered roller was one of these. It was, however, in France that the first steam roller was built, though the development quickly crossed the Channel. Aveling began manufacture of his own engines at Rochester, Kent, in 1862 and quickly built up a commanding position in the field which his company never really lost. In 1867, Aveling introduced the first production road roller, sending the first example to his agent in Paris and another to Liverpool. Subsequently, rollers of this type were sent all over the world. Two of them became the first steam rollers in the United States, helping build, among other projects, the roads in Central Park, New York. The first rollers were far from the shape and layout we now take for granted, being in essence the other way round with the engine unit having the chimney at the rear. There was still a large roller at the front and two larger rollers at the back on each side. A key feature is that the track of the front roll overlaps the rear rolls slightly to allow a full width pass to be made when engaged in rolling. They were 25–30 tons in weight and the machine was steered by a ship's wheel arrangement.

In 1870, Aveling and William Batho published *On a Steam Road Roller*, a paper to the Institution of Mechanical Engineers on the engineering and practicality of these machines. The original design of Aveling-Batho roller was illustrated profusely in drawings and diagrams in this; the design is sometimes known as the 'Birmingham' roller due to having been made for that city initially. A Birmingham roller survived into the 1930s working in the Elan Valley in Mid-Wales and was visited, recorded and photographed by members of the Road Locomotive Society in the closing years of that decade. Sadly it did not survive the Second World War, though the images remain for posterity. Preservation of old steam rollers was not in vogue at the time, though two decades later, it began to take off.

Not long after the construction of the Birmingham rollers, practicality won out as the vehicles were too heavy, and the conventional layout of forward-facing chimney with driver to the rear emerged. Initially a number of these smaller rollers had conical front rolls attached to a tall pin linked to a forecarriage on the smokebox of the engine's boiler. Before long the cast headstock which would characterise the Aveling roller was adopted and then parallel

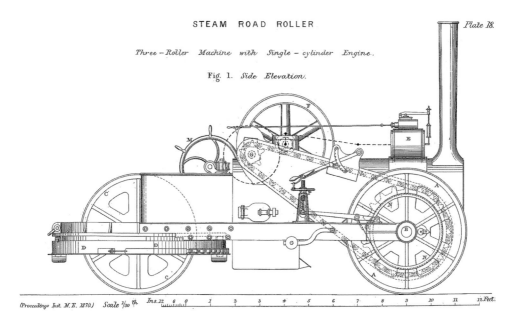

The first drawing of the Batho roller in the paper presented to the Institute of Mechanical Engineers in 1870. By this time Aveling and Batho had fallen out and gave their parts of the paper separately!

An engraving of an Aveling-Batho roller, giving an impression of the size and massive construction of the machine.

rather than tapered rolls were developed. The conical rolls were meant to have a differential effect but were more of a headache than an assistance, and the fact that three-point rollers were made until recent years shows the efficacy of the layout. The weight of the rollers was also reduced to a more practical range of 8–15 tons in general. How it actually works is a basic steam engine on road wheels as described in the author's companion volume in the series, *Traction Engines*.

The classic shape of an Aveling & Porter steam roller evolved in the 1870s; here's an advert for one from the *Land Agents' Record* of March 1896.

Did you know?

Although throughout history Aveling's works has been recorded as being in Rochester in Kent, it was actually situated across the River Medway in Strood.

2

The Heyday of the
Steam Roller

Steam rollers were made in all sizes and configurations for different applications and even locations – not all were made for rolling roads as we expect them and some even rolled diamonds. Being close relatives of the traction engine, the basic layout of parts was similar, though boilers and cylinders were usually suited to slow speeds and gentle steam production rather than hard sustained effort. Some commonality of parts between types of engine occurred with a number of manufacturers – our Aveling roller shares many parts with an 8 hp traction engine. Other rollers were built as convertibles, meaning they could be altered between roller and steam tractor with ease, giving two machines for the price of one and an asset which could find useful employment throughout the year. A few of these engines survive with both sets of parts, though many are now in tractor form only due to owners enjoying the speed and comfort a tractor can bring! As with the traction engine, different weights and

This Aveling machine is a convertible – able to be changed between roller and steam tractor form. Seen at a sale at Les Lambe's yard at Bromsgrove in the 1960s the engine dates from the 1920s, when Aveling used piston valve cylinders.

The smallest steam roller in the world? Arthur Trotter's One Ton roller for use at home has now been restored to steam and is pictured at one of the Great Dorset Steam Fairs.

horsepowers were available, as were other detail options. These included the single-cylinder or compound configuration, the latter giving greater efficiency.

The smallest steam roller made is believed to be the unique 1-ton roller made by Arthur Trotter of Coleford for use on the paths around his home. It was made in 1933 and has a vertical boiler. Upon Trotter's death, it passed to the Gloucester Folk Museum and has recently been lent out for restoration back to working order, a task completed in 2017. The roller turns heads wherever it goes, but is far from a model, being built for a job of work – well worth looking out for.

By and large, the range of weights of steam rollers varied from 6 tons to 15, though the Wallis & Steevens 'Simplicity' was more like 3 tons. Aveling & Porter's range went through many permutations, the largest rollers of 15–20 tons being older machines where deadweight compacting of hardcore or Telford and Macadam roads was important. As road building methods changed, the heavy rollers fell out of favour, the last 15-tonners being made around the end of the First World War. The majority of production was 8 and 10-ton steam rollers, with a number of 12-ton engines in addition. 8-tonners were good for finishing and dressing, 10 and 12-ton rollers were the norm for general road construction. The old 15-ton and above rollers remained for heavy use and the airfield construction of runways in the 1940s saw many commandeered for rolling the hardcore again. Likewise, the old 15-ton Aveling from the 1890s that our family look after was used on the dualling of the Great North Road in Newcastle in the 1950s, showing the usefulness of it even at that late date. How many pieces of modern plant equipment would have such longevity and usefulness now?

In the 1920s, Aveling & Porter moved towards using piston valves on their steam rollers for greater efficiency, but drivers didn't always get on with them, so by 1930 the company went back to the older slide valve style of engine despite being on the verge of becoming part of Aveling-Barford, who made piston-valve rollers to a Ruston design thereafter. The design remained almost the same throughout the 1940s and into the 1950s, with the very last steam roller for the UK market being supplied in 1953. Aveling had attempted to make a new development of steam roller for inferior fuel supplies and the export market in the late 1940s, using many interchangeable parts from the existing G series motor rollers, but this

Above: There can be no better depiction of the variety of Aveling rollers over the decades in terms of size and appearance than this picture of a quartet of rollers on the National Traction Engine Trust's sixtieth anniversary road run from September 2014, led by Dick Blenkinsop's Aveling-Barford of 1937.

Below: Illustrative of the heavy rollers used on Telford and Macadam roads is Alex Sharphouse's 1896 15-tonner, which is displayed at Old Hall Farm in Bouth, Cumbria.

Above: The later Aveling & Porter piston valved compound roller is shown to good effect at the Museum of Science & Industry in Manchester in August 2010 in this beautifully presented example.
Below: Rhondda Council ran an Aveling-Barford, which ran into the 1960s. It was photographed in a typical Valleys scene by David Mitchell around 1962.

was not taken into production. It was somehow fitting given Aveling's place at the inception of the steam roller that they would be there right at the close of steam production.

Rollers, on request of the customer, were also fitted with differential gears to assist with cornering, winch drums on back axles and governors for use when driving static machinery such as stone crushers. This gave greater flexibility to the roller as a piece of machinery, and winches were particularly useful in hilly country where, with an anchor point, they could be used to assist the engine's ascent and descent of the gradient. There are amazing pictures of rollers in Cumbria on some of the mountain passes which defy the imagination – and the crews worked them on a daily basis like this!

A further piece of equipment fitted to many steam rollers, and latterly to some heavier diesel rollers, was the scarifier. Designed to pull up the old road surface and break it up, the scarifier had a number of teeth or tines which could be wound down to the desired depth and pulled through the old road, which could be cleared away and levelled before a new surface was prepared and laid. Bomford & Evershed created their own pattern of scarifier; there was also the Morrison-Rutty patent and a number of others. There was even the Thackray patent, which was a trailer scarifier pulled behind a roller. Scarifying was hard work on an engine and would put immense strain on the bearings, gears and back axle of a roller; our own machine had damage on the right side bearings from many years' working life and uneven wear on other parts.

McLaren of Leeds steam rollers are few and far between in terms of survivors. This one attended the McLaren-themed display at the Great Dorset Steam Fair in September 2010. It has a spoked flywheel and many similarities with the same maker's traction engines.

A further maker of steam rollers was Armstrong Whitworth; their engines were solidly made though unfavourable comparisons were made with Avelings. This one was new to Bishop Auckland Urban District Council and after travelling all over in preservation, it returned to the North East in October 2016 and was soon put to use rolling a farm track.

Road-making techniques evolved with the rollers – if the road for repair or making was a secondary route, what was called a water-bound method would suffice. Broken or small stones formed the base of the road, and these were compacted by a roller passing back and forth until the base was level. Sifted earth was then added which had water mixed in to become a slurry, then rolled level and left to dry. The result was a hard level surface and the late nineteenth century version of the macadam road, which served into the era of the motor car, though heavy lorries and buses wore the road away and created clouds of dust in summer. In towns this was treated by water carts spraying the roads to lay the dust. In country areas this was far from a practical proposition, so another solution was needed.

Just before the First World War, the macadam road was improved by the use of bitumen, asphalt or tar as binding agents. By way of explanation, asphalt is generally a naturally occurring bitumen – an oil-based material, usually already mixed with some fine material in its natural state. There was a big 'lake' in Trinidad which was mined and this was used in the early days from about 1850. Tar is a by-product of the manufacture of gas by burning coal, which was available in quantities as town gas became a popular fuel in urban areas. It was thus initially cheap and thus popular well into the 1970s, falling off as natural gas took over. Later, refined bitumen as a product of the fractional distillation of crude oil became popular and superseded coal tar from the 1960s. With sand and limestone added, this provided a hard and waterproof road surface more resilient to wear. The ingredients were heated and then poured over a prepared macadam surfaced; a dressing of stone chippings was spread over that base and the whole lot compressed by a steam roller. The tar then set, leaving the stones embedded in the tar to form a hardwearing, waterproof and dust-free surface; the technique became known as tar-spraying or tar-bound macadam. In Britain there was a huge push to tar-spray rural roads in the 1920s and 1930s, and a rise in contractors such as Woods, Box's, Bridson's, Isaac Ball and Mechanical Tar Spraying & Grouting, etc. A lot of money was made! Nowadays this process is still widely used, essentially for two reasons – it waterproofs the road surface, but the main reason is that a layer of surface dressing restores the skid resistance of a surface.

In the 1930s, crushed slag from iron and steel works was pre-coated with tar away from the work site and delivered to location, ready-mixed in hot form. This was given the trade name Tarmac and was then carried by men with forks and spread into place to form what became known as a metalled road surface. The steam roller levelled it and men standing by with shovels of tarmac filled depressions that formed as the roller worked. To prevent the sticky tarred stones clinging to the rollers, most were now either made or later fitted with a water spray to keep the rolls wet and stop the tar from sticking. Similarly, scrapers were fitted which ran close to the rolls to remove any stones that had become stuck.

Tarmac needs lighter and faster rollers. The Wallis Advance and Marshall Universal were lighter at between 6 and 10 tons, faster and quick reversing, giving no dwell time on the hot asphalt and a smooth road surface. Their engines were twin high-pressure units with no

Marshall's answer to the need for evenly weighted fast rollers on tarmac was the Universal type with enclosed engine and other innovative features. Few remain; this one appeared at the 1984 Town & Country Festival in Warwickshire, where two years previously it was the first steam roller the author ever drove.

The Advance was the successful later roller made by Wallis & Steevens with a twin cylinder engine for quick reversing. The picture shows the very first of its type at the Onslow Park Rally near Shrewsbury in August 2007.

flywheel, adding to their versatility, and the back axle could also camber to follow the road surface. The Advance rollers could also have their rolls changed to alter the weight laid down on the road surface. The weight distribution of a roller on tarmac is important; one needs equal pressure on the front and back rolls. Modern 'tarmac' is in its simplest form a mix of quarried aggregate and bitumen.

Away from the typical rollers, a number of oddities appeared. The Mann Patent Steam Cart Company of Leeds built some patching rollers based on the mechanics of their existing steam carts, and one remains in preservation. The Wallis & Steevens 3-ton Simplicity with an inclined boiler was designed for export use with inferior fuel. Six of these quirky little rollers survive in the UK, with one in the USA. They have an appeal of their own, and in good order one was even roaded over 12 miles to a Midlands rally in 2006! Tandem Robey and Tri-Tandem 'Waveless' rollers were similarly designed with the purpose of even weight distribution and smooth tarmac laying. The Tri-Tandems were three conversions by third parties with components supplied by Robeys as the company was unwilling to do the work themselves. These rollers survived in use until quite late – it is suggested that one was used on part of the construction of the M1 motorway – and two survive into preservation. Aveling & Porter also made a tandem type, as did Armstrong Whitworth. Luton Museums own a rare conventional layout tandem, while a further Aveling oddity is the side-engined roller known to enthusiasts as the 'Shay' type, due to the similarity to the American railway locomotives developed by Ephraim Shay. A similar tandem roll configuration is used, but the steam engine drive is mounted vertically to the side of the boiler and drives through bevel gears to the back axle. A similar configuration was developed by American builders such as Iroquois and Buffalo Springfield, though these had vertical boilers.

Vertical-boilered rollers were mainly the preserve of American manufacturers on the whole, and with a very strong home construction base, imported steam rollers didn't really happen – it was only later with diesel road rollers that non-UK builders began to make inroads into the market, with Galion and Huber coming in during the Second World War (as Lend-Lease), and Hamm much later. A couple of UK builders did make vertical-boilered steam rollers though: Barford in the 1880s and then Aveling & Porter in the late 1920s made some, as did Marshalls of Gainsborough, again to the tandem layout. The Marshalls had steam-powered steering too, in an attempt to make the driver's life more bearable – the poetic description of a steam roller 'dreamily steered by an elderly toiler' being very far from the reality. Any attempt to ease working conditions would be welcomed and was also a move towards being real opposition to the newer internal combustion rollers being introduced at that time.

Patching rollers were made for repairs rather than roadmaking, the Mann Patent Steam Cart Company of Leeds being responsible for this example of the type.

Wallis & Steeven's Simplicity model roller was made for use with poor fuel and its sloping boiler was intended to give good steam raising capability; six are left in preservation. The author's daughter Charlotte is driving the roller in this picture while she was taking part in a Steam Apprentice Club Driving Day.

Dave Riley has done a fine job of restoring his Robey Tandem roller. The boiler is of a unique design for ease of maintenance and the rollers have a very distinctive appearance.

The Robey Tri-Tandem was an in-service modification to the Tandem to suit the user's needs. Two remain in preservation and certainly draw plenty of attention at the rallies they attend.

The Aveling & Porter tandem is represented by this sole survivor, made new for Luton Corporation. By September 2006 it was part of the collection of Luton Museums Service, who showed it at the Bedford Steam Rally.

Another unusual Aveling roller is the side engine Shay-type roller. With an ungainly appearance, it is a rare survivor, and worked for the well-known firm of Buncombe in commercial service.

The contrast between vertical boiler and conventional rollers is clear in this photo from the August 2013 Great Dorset Steam Fair. The Aveling on the left was visiting from Holland, but similar rollers operated in the UK.

Most steam traction engine manufacturers made rollers, even if it wasn't in huge numbers – the market was dominated though by Aveling & Porter, Fowler, Marshall and Wallis & Steevens, with Aveling being right at the head of the field, a fact reflected in the number of surviving steam rollers of their manufacture in the preservation scene. Burrells of Thetford, Clayton & Shuttleworth of Lincoln and Thomas Green of Leeds also made a number of rollers, while some of the big steam manufacturers made few or no rollers at all. Some contractors favoured one make or type while others mixed their fleets, making the study of their operations fascinating as one follows the favoured make of one chief engineer or borough surveyor then to another company perhaps as personnel change. The determination of some to stay with steam is also quite marked, with a number keeping steam rollers in operation well into the 1960s.

There seems to be a tie-in between some of the manufacturers and some of the larger contractors; there was certainly a tie-in with Woods of Yeadon and Fowlers. It has been suggested that Norman Box's business, Box Tar Spraying & Grouting, was partially financed by Fowlers. It's possible that so too was the Mechanical Tar Spraying & Grouting business in Reading given the almost entirely Fowler-only equipment used.

CHARLES BURRELL & SONS, LIMITED, THETFORD, ENGLAND.

ROAD ROLLER FITTED WITH SINGLE CYLINDER.

Manufacturers were keen to sell their wares and engines were given a special show finish. Burrell's were renowned for their high standard of turnout, as this catalogue image of one of their single-cylinder rollers demonstrates.

Above: Fowlers of Leeds built robust and dependable steam rollers; Lloyd Jones Brothers of Llanfair DC, Ruthin, were working this example on a building site in 1973.
Below: Steaming away from the Burton-on-Trent Museum of Brewing in March 2008 is this Clayton & Shuttleworth roller and road train. Clayton rollers were solid and well-engineered and this example has a very good reputation for excellent performance in preservation.

Right: One of the lesser represented manufacturers of steam rollers is Thomas Green of Leeds. Of distinctive appearance, this example calls Bury Transport Museum home.

Below: Allchin steam rollers only have two survivors in preservation; the only working one appeared at Beamish Museum in April 2014, a very welcome sight to compare with some of the more usual makes.

STEAM ROLLER AT WORK

Tom Charman photographed Devon County Council's Marshall roller, fleet number 132, at work on Dartmoor near Princetown on 28 August 1965.

Did you know?

As well as the well-known traction engine manufacturers undertaking the building of steam rollers, some of the railway locomotive builders had a go at joining the market. These included Manning Wardle of Leeds who made a steam road roller around 1869, which then was known to have operated until around 1875. It's not believed that they dabbled any more in the market, leaving steam rollers in Leeds the preserve of Fowlers and Greens.

3
Young Pretenders

The first motor rollers saw light at the start of the twentieth century in both the UK and on the Continent. Barford & Perkins made some in Britain while French and German makers built some in the first decade of the century. Petrol rollers were the mainstay of Barford's production from 1904, based initially on their range of agricultural rollers fitted with engines. Thus lightweight rollers were made in Peterborough for another thirty years, for use as both grass and road rollers, the Type A being perhaps the best known. Like the steam roller, many of these were long-lived, a good number finding their way to a second life as cricket pitch rollers once they were replaced by their council or contractor owners. Some were re-engined with car engines and ran into the 1990s; the author bought one in 2000 from Market Drayton Cricket Club for £40, fitted with a Vauxhall Chevette car engine! Others remained original until the end, such as the 1929 version operated into the last decade of the twentieth century at Warwick Cricket Club. Their long lives were reflected in the large number of Type A rollers which have survived into enthusiast and museum possession, and when fully restored with original brass radiator shroud, they make a very attractive sight indeed. Great fun to drive with a hand reverse

Barford & Perkins were making petrol motor rollers before the First World War. One of the oldest survivors appeared at the Great North Steam Fair at Beamish in April 2015. No frills or fripperies towards the aesthetics of the machine!

Many contractors operating steam roller fleets were quick to catch on with motor rollers. In June 2017, there was a reunion of rollers from the fleet of Isaac Ball of Wharles in Lancashire and it was good to see this Barford & Perkins Pioneer taking its place in the display.

Barford & Perkins Type A motor rollers are very attractive preservation projects; two nicely restored examples lead the display of motor rollers at the 2013 Great Dorset Steam Fair where the special theme was road rollers.

and throttle, the driver is instantly at one with the machine from priming the cylinders on the engine to hand cranking it to start – almost as physical a challenge as a steam roller!

In the 1930s, a subsidiary of the Singer Motor Company was set up called Motor Units of Coventry. This latter firm made Villiers engine-powered petrol rollers for patching and paving; they weighed only 10 hundredweight each and could be bought for £45 in 1936. Variations on this rollers include a pedal-powered version, which must have been good exercise! Earlier in the century, Thomas Green of Leeds had made an electric-powered roller using an overhead power cable like a tram, though to my knowledge, this has so far been a unique application of electricity to road rolling.

The first diesel roller in Britain was made by Aveling & Porter in 1923. The best known type is perhaps the Aveling Barford DX with its single-cylinder Ruston or Blackstone engine, followed by the Barford SD9 with a distinctive red livery ex works. Ruston & Hornsby of Lincoln made their own oil-engined rollers too, but these were not as widespread as the Aveling single-cylinder rollers, whose construction spanned two decades. Very distinctive machines with air start to turn the engine over to a speed where it will run on diesel power, the DX and DY pattern rollers are still sought out by preservationists today and for many are almost steam rollers in their mind's eye with external flywheels and exhaust note.

Builders who made steam rollers did not necessarily make the move to motor rollers and vice versa – much was tied up in the ill-fated Agricultural & General Engineering Combine (an engineering co-operative of sorts, created to try and get through hard trading times) – the largest roller manufacturer to weather the depression of the 1920s was the amalgamation of Aveling & Porter with Barford & Perkins to form Aveling-Barford. The diesel roller did not readily displace the steam roller despite its greater efficiency. One of the reasons behind

The Aveling-Barford DX and DY single-cylindered diesel rollers are very characterful and a welcome sight on many rally fields. This well-travelled example was at Preston in Kent after a rally there in July 2008.

Above: In the Cumbrian hills is the Threlkeld Quarry Museum, where this Barford & Perkins SD9 resides. In full working order, it is often used in working demonstrations around the museum site.
Below: At the end of Aveling & Porter's existence, before they became part of Aveling-Barford, a number of Blackstone-engined heavy oil rollers were made. Not many are seen at events; in 2009 this one was resident in County Durham and was taking part in a roadmaking display at Beamish.

this was that the steam engine was built to a very high standard, and thus over-engineered, lasting for years – for example, the Aveling steam roller the author looks after ran from the 1890s to 1960s, a not untypical feat for many rollers. There were also very large numbers of steam rollers; a county council or contractor with dozens or more of them would not take the decision to replace them when good steam coal was cheap. A steam roller could be relied upon to give years of trouble-free service from new, whereas a diesel roller needed continuous maintenance of injectors and fuel pumps. Also, the newer technology of the oil or petrol engine was not as simple as the basic steam engine to maintain. Eventually the rising cost of coal, the need for water supplies and the long working day raising steam before being ready for use tipped the balance in favour of the diesel roller, but mostly throughout the 1940s and '50s, a considerable time after steam on the road and on the farm had already entered decline. The legacy of the steam roller was the fact that they had rolled the majority of the British road network between the wars – but change was on its way.

In the 1930s through to the 1950s, a number of steam rollers were converted with diesel or petrol engines to extend their working lives after boiler failures; a number of these were undertaken by Bomford & Evershed, the well-known engineers and roller contractors of Salford Priors in Warwickshire, who ran an extensive fleet of rollers into the 1960s as well as making their own living vans for drivers and crews to live in when on jobs or out on the road. A number of Bomford steam rollers are now preserved, while a couple of the diesel

Originally built in 1887 as a steam roller, when the boiler needed replacing Bomford & Evershed re-engineered this old Aveling with a McLaren diesel engine and extended its working life. Now beautifully restored by Mark Vine, it turns heads at any event it attends.

conversions still exist, one being the wonderfully restored example with Mark Vine in Essex, who is not afraid to road and demonstrate his machine. It draws interest wherever it goes, being a rebuild of a venerable 1887 steam roller in the first case.

During the Second World War, rollers found use in airfield construction and repair, but the manufacture of machinery was also restricted. Utility rollers became a requirement, being made with Fordson tractor engines and other mechanics by Aveling-Barford. They were fast and fairly light to cope with rolling the length of runways. Raw materials were scarce and the rolls themselves were filled with concrete to compensate for the lack of metal in the machine. They were expendable pieces of equipment, but Aveling-Barford, used to producing quality machines, was appalled at having to compromise its standards. To protect their reputation and with an eye to post-war sales, the company embossed all the castings of the machine with 'War Design' to act as an apologia. The Royal Air Force had its own Airfield Construction Branch from 1941 to 1966 with a number of plant depots around the country where rollers were based. The author's own Wallis & Steevens Advance diesel roller was built new in 1944 for the Air Ministry and sold into civilian use in 1960, when it was registered for the road with Warwickshire County Council. It continued with a contractor in Leamington Spa until the 1970s – a not untypical situation for many pieces of redundant plant.

Starting life with the Air Ministry in 1944, the author's 2.5-ton Wallis & Steevens Advance is typical of many rollers which worked for the services in the Second World War. Sold into civilian service in 1960, it returned to Leamington and Warwick in July 2014 and was displayed here on the games field at Warwick School for their 1,100th anniversary!

Did you know?

To allow different widths to be rolled, the small Wallis & Steevens diesel and petrol Advance rollers had removable and reversible rear rolls to allow for wider or narrower tracks to be traversed as the roller ran back and forth.

Rollers could have their weight increased through the innovation of water-filled rolls, something pioneered by Barford & Perkins in 1888 but very much taken into vogue with motor rollers. Marshalls and Wallis & Steevens moved with the times and made many diesel rollers into the late twentieth century. Wallis went from water-cooled engines with hand start and mechanical gearboxes to air-cooled engines with hydraulic drive, and were still making rollers until the works was closed in 1981. At the sale of the Basingstoke premises, the historic collection of rollers was also sold, Wallis & Steevens having assembled a number of their past products to commemorate their production. These included Advance and Simplicity steam rollers, the latter of which, after passing through enthusiast hands, is now in the Milestones Museum in Basingstoke, where there is a reconstruction of part of the Wallis works. An 8-ton diesel Advance is also part of the display, allowing direct comparisons to be made between the types.

Bringing motor rollers into the 1980s, this diesel-hydraulic Wallis & Steevens roller was entered in the Cheffins Vintage Auction in Cambridgeshire in April 2014. The covers on the rear rolls that can be removed to add water and increase weight can be clearly seen.

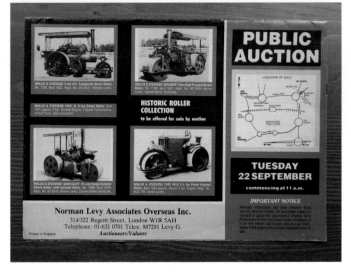

Some of the long-established firms of roller manufacturers had their own collections of historic artefacts. So it was with Wallis & Steevens, and this is part of the sale brochure for when they finally closed and sold up the works.

Aveling-Barford rose to eminence after the Second World War with their G series of rollers, the GA being the smallest, moving up through to the GD at the largest, later leading the way to the Master Pavior model. Rubber-tyred rollers came in through the 1960s, but the dead weight three-point roller with its origins in the Master Pavior was made right through to the last days of Aveling-Barford in the ownership of Wordsworth Holdings in 1996. There was always something reassuring about seeing the trademark rampant horse in brass on the front of the roller, despite them having been made in Lincolnshire since the 1930s when the works moved from Kent. The sloping bonnet of the Aveling lasted throughout production, although comfort for the driver went from a steam-style awning on upright pillars to an enclosed cab during the 1950s.

The world of road rollers cannot ignore the pedestrian-controlled pavement or patching rollers either, though in heritage terms, it is certain that these are very much the forgotten relations of the road-making world. For work between that which small rollers can cope with and the pneumatic hand-held tamping and packing devices, the hand roller was very much ideal. Initially a self-propelled single roller, they developed into the vibrating roller whose action multiplied the compression applied to the road surface. Sisis and Stothert & Pitt made the market very much their own, the latter also making a version with a second roll and driving position to make them ride-on machines. In recent times the hand-controlled roller has become the preserve of Mortimer Vibroll in Rutland, whose products are simple to run and easy to maintain, ensuring their place in the manufacturers' market in the twenty-first century.

The traditional look of the Aveling-Barford Master Pavior and GD-type roller lasted from the 1960s to the 1990s, and examples can still be found at work today. In October 2008 this example was working in Porthmadog, Gwynedd, and still carried the Aveling badge on the front.

Above: More useful for compacting hardcore, this Aveling-Barford combined steel and rubber-tyred roller dates from the 1960s and is in a collection of classic plant and machinery in the West Midlands.
Below: Overlooked by many, the pedestrian controlled roller is good for patching repairs and pavement work. In the foreground is a Sisis machine and behind it a later Benford item.

Stothert & Pitt of Bath are well-known as crane makers, but turned their hand to vibrating rollers in the 1960s. Hand-controlled ones were adapted to become self-propelled, and a preserved example was part of the road making display at the Great Dorset Steam Fair in 2017, contrasting sharply with its steam-powered neighbours.

Did you know?

Even the contractor Eddisons got in on the roller building act, creating the diesel-hydraulic 'Eddimatic' in the 1960s and building the prototype in their works, though the production models were made by Thomas Green of Leeds. Today, only the prototype survives, in the collections of Leicester Museums.

Some oddities were made over time, one being the bizarre marriage by an enterprising user of a Ruston & Hornsby narrow gauge diesel locomotive with a Robey tandem steam roller chassis to make a diesel roller. Somewhat more planned was the Twose of Tiverton Tractoroller. Twose are more often known for agricultural rollers but in the 1950s they created a road roller that allowed a conventional farm tractor to turn into a road roller by driving it onto an underframe and using a chain drive to make the contraption mobile. Equally different was the Road-Marshall, a conversion of a Field Marshall single-cylinder tractor into a roller. How the Field Marshall performed with its distinctive engine beat is not recorded, but at least one of these machines survives in preservation, as do a couple of Twose rollers.

Above: The Field-Marshall tractor is a distinctive single-cylinder beast. Not so well-known is its roller derivative, the Road-Marshall; this one is kept in a private collection in Lincolnshire.

Right: Eric Smith of Swillington Rollers has a habit of taking a roller to the venue of the Road Roller Association Annual General Meeting every year. In 2017 he took this Keynsham roller to the hotel in Ulverston just before lunch for all to see.

While the road roller may not be a piece of plant made by large manufacturers in the UK, one business remains producing small rollers for the modern user with a view to the past as well. Although the main business of Swillington Rollers near Leeds is now to provide rollers for grass pitches, many of their products began life as small road rollers which have been re-engineered and made suitable for modern operation. New designs have also been introduced, but the proprietors have sought out derelict rollers in need of repair, rebuilding and refurbishing them for new owners. Swillington's own-brand 'Supreme' model offers the modern groundsman everything they need. There is even a thriving export strand to the company, which is run by roller enthusiast Eric Smith, his wife Marlene and his son Simon. It goes without saying that Eric is an avid member of the Road Roller Association and often takes his latest roller to display at the Association's Annual General Meeting.

Not far from the author's home, we were able to watch rollers at work with Rainton Construction in County Durham during January and February 2018. There were Hamm three-point and tandem rollers together, the three-point weighing 10 tons and being eighteen years old and no longer in production by Hamm and the 3 to 4-ton vibrating drum tandem roller, which has the impact of a 10-tonner with the vibrating action enabled. The process of rolling tarmac may be highly mechanised now, but there is still a large team spreading chippings and using the spreader, rake and shovels, only the waistcoats and flat caps have been replaced by hard hats and high visibility orange overalls. This work is still repeated on a daily basis across the UK, keeping roadmaking and road rollers in the public eye – and helps maintain the term 'steam roller' in everyday language.

The snow and ice of February 2018 did not stop road works across the country. In Durham, local contractors Rainton were hard at work resurfacing with one of their Hamm three-point rollers, a type no longer made.

4
Working with Rollers

Road-making was a very labour intensive job, and the adoption of the road roller took only a small part of the human element out of the work – though of course it was a very hard part, having had hand or horse rollers previously. There would be many men working on a section of tarmacadam road in the mid-twentieth century, for example. A tar boiler and an asphalt mixer boiler required attention, then men would apply tar using large cans. More of the gang would spread the tar evenly with stiff brushes and then a top dressing of stone chippings was applied in sweeping movements of shovels to ensure an even layer of stones on top of the surface of the molten tar. When the foreman was satisfied that the road had been prepared to his requirement, the steam roller came into play to compact and level the road surface, rolling backwards and forwards, overlapping itself on each pass to ensure full coverage. The old drivers knew of this skill as 'half wheeling'. As the process was mechanised and got faster, the rollers would need to follow the tar and chipping spreading machinery, and the operation became known as 'chipchasing'.

When dressing the virgin stone, the roller driver would 'half wheel' this to shape, making sure his passes over the stone overlapped to make sure no area was missed. In the early days, or on small areas, men would use watering cans of tar obtained from the boiler, then

Tom Galliford and team at Arley near Nuneaton in the early 1920s, a typical rural roadmaking scene such as would have been seen all across the country.

A typical job for Thomas Galliford in the late 1920s, with an Aveling steam roller and Tasker steam waggon moving materials somewhere in North Warwickshire. Note how clean the roller is, even as a piece of working plant.

spread chippings by shovel. However the roller would only run over the chippings in enough passes to embed them, say only once or twice, so that the chippings were not crushed. Later the spreading apparatus was fitted to the tar boiler itself, often in the form of a bar known as a 'flapper'.

Laying tarmac or asphalt would involve the same half rolling preparation of the virgin stone, mixing the material (binder and aggregate), and laying it by men with buckets with the best men on the rake forming the shape, the roller driver finishing it using his skill.

Peter Galliford, former chairman of the company of the same name, now Galliford Try, recalled driving rollers for his father's company in Wolvey in the 1940s while his father was unwell. As a young man moving on in the business, he learned the hard way, dealing with accidents and moving rollers from one job to another over long distances and with some challenging hills! Road rollers don't like steep hills as their smooth rolls have very little grip on the metalled road surface, thus the driver needs to be in complete control throughout a descent of any gradient. Mr Galliford senior went from working for a contractor himself at the same time as driving ploughing engines to buying his own roller and setting up in business in his own right and building a fleet. Despite rising to become a senior captain of industry, Peter bought a Barford roller for fun in the 1990s! He talked of the unique experience of running a wartime Utility roller with Fordson gear box... and the characters who ran the rollers – one particularly sharp-suited gentleman acquired the nickname 'The Spiv' while with Gallifords.

The position was repeated in many locations across the country, as fleets were assembled of steam rollers, living vans and later motor rollers. Living vans for the roller driver were vital as some road-making jobs could see the driver away from home for days if not weeks at a

The sharp-suited driver known as 'The Spiv' poses with his Greens roller, part of Galliford's fleet around 1950.

Isaac Ball of Wharles ran a fleet of steam rollers, all equipped with the full-length roof as seen here, and mostly made by Burrells. They also built their own living vans, such as the one behind the roller. The road train, including the water cart, was part of the Ball reunion event held in June 2017.

time. Some were basic, others were embellished somewhat, but never reached the heights of the showman's van. Vans were made by the same builders as the rollers, but a number of contractors made their own, like Isaac Ball of Wharles or Jacksons of Wistaston, and other manufacturers such as Smiths of Barnard Castle entered the market in their own right, never having made a roller.

Famous company and fleet names such as Bomford & Evershed, Buncombes and Eddisons appeared and ran several dozen rollers each, with Eddison running into the hundreds. They had depots all across the country, at all points of the compass, and often ran rollers between those depots, the delivering driver then having to find his own way back to his home depot. These operators did nothing else, though a number of other companies had fleets of rollers alongside their other business activities such as the builders Dawkins of Westwood Heath near Coventry, whose yard still contained nine vintage motor rollers as late as the early 2000s. Some of the companies had their own house magazine, one of the biggest being Road Rollers Ltd, who solely ran motor rollers from the 1920s on, never owning a steam roller. Workshops could be extensive, and many photographs exist of the facilities of Buncombes of Highbridge, which became a mecca to steam enthusiasts as the fleet was run down but not scrapped. Many rollers were stored in the 1960s and were thus a ready source for the eager preservationist. Likewise Bomford & Evershed of Salford Priors had a large number of stored steam rollers and living vans at the end of the steam period and a good number of these can now be seen on the heritage scene. In a similar way, old diesel rollers continue to be found in yards around the country, often finding their way into preservation as the interest grows. Sentimentality among the former owners can also see

Bomford & Evershed of Salford Priors was a very large contractor at one point and kept steam into the 1960s. The Bomford yard was a happy hunting ground for enthusiasts and preservationists and a good number of Bomford steam rollers and living vans survive into the twenty-first century for all to enjoy.

The house magazine of Road Rollers Limited is a fascinating insight into the workings of the company and the social lives of its employees.

A visit to Addingham in West Yorkshire in November 2015 found a pair of Marshall diesel rollers parked up and looking for new homes. Both were bought by enthusiasts and the one nearest the camera has now been fully restored – and there are still rollers out there to be found.

a machine retained in the back of a property rather than weighed in for the scrap value it can realise – this was recently the case of a pair of 1940s Marshall diesel rollers in Addingham, West Yorkshire, which will now live again in enthusiast hands.

Woods of Yeadon in Yorkshire created their own patent tar spraying and gritting gear, which can be seen on the Craske family's Fowler roller across the Yorkshire rally scene. Likewise, Mechanical Tarspraying & Grouting of Reading had a similar tarspraying set-up on many of their rollers, though once again surviving equipment is rare – it was a pleasure at the 2016 auction of the Keeley collection in Berkshire to see a Fowler T3 roller from the fleet in almost untouched condition. Other contractors developed their own pieces of equipment such as the Bomford scarifier, or adaptations of existing rollers, like the work undertaken by Allens of Oxford with rebuilds and alterations. These could be simple interventions or complete rebuilds and replacements of parts. Maintenance workshops were extensive and as seen earlier, Bomfords also worked on their own conversions of steam rollers into internal combustion machines, with considerable success. Likewise, they built their own living vans for use with the fleet, and Bomford vans are highly prized today.

Away from contractors, many local boards, rural district or urban district councils ran fleets of rollers leading into county councils. Some borough council fleets were absorbed into the larger county councils, and on occasions a contractor would hire in a roller from a council if they hadn't enough or if there was one nearby. Peter Galliford's collection of photographs from the family firm shows images of his father driving for Eddisons, but the rollers are most definitely still plated up for council ownership. The author's Aveling steam roller was with two contractors before purchase by Northumberland County Council. The rise of fleets, councils and contractors saw the slow decline of the owner/operator, with the last of this kind being Lyndon Shearman in Halifax, West Yorkshire, who ran from the 1960s into the 1980s, his final roller – fittingly a Yorkshire-built Greens – now being part of the collection of Leeds Museums at Armley Mills. A few councils retain steam rollers as heritage pieces now, the best known being Devon County Council who have several – Marshall, Aveling and Greens being represented. Other councils have put their rollers into the local museum, but it's surprising to see how many are still owned by local authorities.

Many rollers were well maintained, and their drivers remained with them for decades on occasions – latterly, when a roller was withdrawn from service in the 1950s or '60s, often it wasn't because the roller was worn out but because the driver was retiring and it was hard to find a younger man who was prepared for the working life of a steam roller man. The travelling life with a living van no longer suited a lot of people, and the electric start on a diesel engine won out over an early morning needed for raising steam. Not a job for a family man either in the changing world, or one who wanted job security. A roller driver for Bomfords might find himself laid off due to lack of work and then taken on again at very short notice. A collection of letters from the company in the possession of Matthew Daw reveal just quite how much of a knife-edge an employee might find themselves on; in one letter, the man is asked to fetch a roller back from a job, then within days he is given his cards terminating his employment.

Unusual owners of rollers included estates and railway companies, with the Great Western Railway ordering and operating an Aveling-Barford steam roller right at the end of their existence in 1947 – and it survived long enough in use with British Railways to become the sole preserved example of a railway-operated steam roller.

The Keeley sale in Berkshire will be long remembered for the variety of quality lots that came up for sale, one of the stars being this original Fowler T3 steam roller from the fleet of Reading-based Mechanical Tarspraying & Grouting. Its condition merited a premium price and its return to steam is eagerly awaited.

BOMFORD & EVERSHED Ltd., Salford Priors, Evesham

Please send Wages up to THURSDAY NIGHT as below —

Engine No. 3321   DRIVER'S TIME.   Date .... 19......

(Mark which days.)	Fri.	Sat.	Sun.	Mon.	Tue.	Wed.	Thu.	Fri.	Sat.	Sun.	Mon.	Tue.	Wed.	Thu.	Total	Rate	£	s.	d.
Days Driving	✓	✓		½	✓	✓	✓	✓	✓			✓	✓						
„ Repairing or Washing out				½															
„ Delayed by frost, etc.																			

Unless Postage is entered each Pay Day it will not be paid, as we cannot check it when allowed to run on longer than a fortnight.

Receipted Bills for these payments must be obtained and sent in with this Pay Sheet

Train Fare, from .... to ....
Postage ....
Coal Bills ....
Blacksmith's Bills ....
Washing Bills ....
Carriage on Empties, etc. ....
Other Expenses ....

Sweeper's Name ....   SWEEPER'S TIME.

(Mark which days.)	Fri.	Sat.	Sun.	Mon.	Tue.	Wed.	Thu.	Fri.	Sat.	Sun.	Mon.	Tue.	Wed.	Thu.	Total	Rate
Days Sweeping																
„ Repairing or Washing out																	
„ Delayed by frost etc.																	

Name ....

Less Cash received on account (if any)

Total due .... £

FULL ADDRESS WHERE MONEY IS TO BE SENT.

Write your ENGINE NUMBER plainly on all Coal Tickets and Bills, and enclose same with this Pay Sheet.
Do NOT write orders for stores and other communications on this Sheet; use the post cards and letter paper provided.

Bomford & Evershed was a major employer and roller operator, and this driver's time sheet in the collection of Matthew Daw gives an insight into the job of steam roller driver in the 1930s.

Throughout the 1960s, the sight of a working steam roller became rarer. Merioneth County Council was one local authority that kept steam on until the late 1960s, when Robert Mitchell caught one of the Council's Fowlers at work at Llangelynin, between Tywyn and Llwyngwril.

British Railways inherited a number of steam rollers and associated tackle from the Great Western Railway, which transported them around the network on special wagons. Most were taken out of service in the 1950s; this Marshall was seen by Tom Charman on Swindon Works dump around that time, the damage to its roof having been caused by rough unloading with a crane.

Did you know?

The steam roller lasted at work in the UK long enough for examples to be used in the building of the M1 motorway alongside new bulldozers and other plant. The very last commercially operated steam roller with a council finished work in the 1980s. Lloyd-Jones Brothers of Ruthin were also using working steam rollers into the 1980s alongside a Sentinel steam waggon used for tar spraying.

An incongruous sight captured by Mike Jones in 1973 was Lloyd-Jones Bros' Fowler roller No. 21628 and their Sentinel tarspraying steam waggon alongside modern plant at Llanbedr Hall, Llanbedr DC.

5
What Next?

It takes a certain kind of madness to preserve a road roller, steam, diesel or petrol-powered. All are heavy and awkward and the amount of time, effort and money expended upon restoration or repairs is not reflected in the value of the machine at the end of the work. Yet it is fun, and the roller folk are a particularly sociable type. In recent years, road-making demonstrations have taken off and become popular, with all manner of supporting equipment from living vans to tar boilers, lamps and road repair signs. Working demonstrations such as these are immensely popular and as good as any working museum when done well.

In 1966, the author's father and his friends Trevor Daw, Doug Kempton and Gus Palmer all clubbed together, forming the Arden Steam Group, to buy a derelict Ruston & Hornsby steam roller. They paid £100 for the compound engine, which was lying at the Bransford Bear public house in Worcestershire. The Group had connections with the Hockley Heath Steam Association and the Warwickshire Steam Engine Society, so the plan was made to take it home to their county – under its own steam. Over a period of twelve months, the roller was retubed with no power tools and fettled to make it roadworthy to travel to Hockley Heath,

Ruston & Hornsby steam roller No. 114059 under repair by the Arden Steam Group at the Bransford Bear pub in Worcestershire. Despite the primitive conditions, the roller would steam home the following year!

In finally restored form, the Ruston roller was rallied and shown by Trevor Daw extensively throughout the West Midlands in the 1980s and 1990s, usually travelling under its own steam.

The appeal of preserving steam has seen many hundreds of steam rollers saved for posterity at all sorts of locations. John Wilkins bought two Wallis & Steevens Advance rollers from Davies Brothers of Barmouth and kept them at the Fairbourne Railway, where they were noted under repair in the late 1960s.

A popular event for steam rollers from the 1960s to 1990s was the Birmingham Science Museum rally; on 18 May 1969, Laurence Watts was taking his Aveling roller home from the event. The roller had spent its working life with ICI at Witton in Birmingham and remains a popular rally attender today, albeit under different ownership with Fred Cooper in Berkshire.

and in March 1967 the Ruston set sail under its own steam and would later grace many rally fields over the following decades in the ownership of Trevor Daw and now the Vickery family.

I'd like therefore to offer a short personal look at over twenty years of preserving rollers. The first one came in 1996 when a 1944 Wallis & Steevens diesel roller was rescued from Victoria Park in Leamington Spa, my home town. After a number of days' work with my friend Ken Milns, we got it going again over the Easter weekend in 1998. Around ten years later, the roller was borrowed by Trevor Daw, our family friend from the 1960s, and he completely rebuilt it in his workshop.

The diesel roller and experience gained from its rehabilitation led to a steam roller, and the 15-ton Aveling No. 3315 of 1894 joined the fleet in the summer of 2003. Having stood idle since being taken out of service in the 1950s, it had lost a number of parts, but the boiler was in essence good, and friends assured us that the rest of the machine could be repaired or replaced. New skills were learned such as rivetting, welding, gas cutting and tubing the boiler. As with any restoration, there were setbacks, but with steady fundraising and the help of many friends, progress was made. In 2012, the roller lived again, taking its first moves at a party to celebrate the restoration and support given by so many. The whole family love it and the fun and friendship it has brought to us all.

Running a roller on the road also requires the driver to hold a Category G driving licence; a group of friends and myself took our tests on one day together on the Milns family's Aveling convertible GND steam roller *Lady Hesketh*. We all passed, but it is possible to take the test on a motor roller if a steam one is not available, or your cup of tea. Without a Category G licence, one needs to display 'L' plates out on the public highway.

The two rollers in the care of the author – an 1894 Aveling & Porter 15-ton machine and the 1944 Wallis & Steevens diesel Advance of much lighter weight. One of the few times both have ever been seen together was a party in July 2012 to mark the first steaming of the Aveling since the 1950s at the now-closed Vintage Vehicles Museum in Shildon, Co. Durham.

The author took his Category G driving test on this Aveling convertible roller. Another popular activity is to take rollers back to where they once worked, and in the summer of 1996, *Lady Hesketh* made a return to its working area of Aberystwyth, where it was engaged in building a new church car park at St Michael's.

Did you know?

Social media is everywhere these days, but a surprising number of rollers and ancillary equipment are bought and sold by it now. The author's water cart came out of Hampshire after a post on a Facebook page by the owner of a narrow gauge steam railway locomotive!

A living van is a particularly sociable aspect of preservation, being based around living, eating and sleeping together. Research into a good restoration can involve the whole family, and even if you're not an engineer, the work in a living van encompasses interior design, woodwork and paintwork. Some people return the van to its original condition, others make the vehicle a real home from home, with modern commodities hidden behind period features. Likewise, some vans are kept on their original iron or steel wheels, though the addition of solid rubber tyres or even pneumatic ones reduces the risk to the crockery when in transit. A stove or small cooking range completes the ensemble and ensures comfort on a cool autumn evening at an end of season event.

While a steam roller is quite an investment, even in a derelict condition – and takes quite a bit of effort to move around – in recent years, the rise of interest in motor roller preservation has rather taken off. It's true the larger models such as the Aveling Barford DX or DY types and the Barford & Perkins SD9 require low-loaders to move them, but the small patching or path rollers around 2 tons in weight can be towed on a good plant trailer behind a Land Rover. Their ease of starting and ready availability, which made them such useful pieces of plant, has made them very desirable pieces of heritage equipment and a well restored small roller will now fetch £2–3,000 at the time of writing. Rollers in need of love can be bought for much cheaper and kept in a domestic garage or on a home drive! It's addictive and great fun.

In the preservation era there has been a trend in the past to convert steam rollers into forms that they never worked in, such as steam tractors or showman's engines, and while this has seen over a hundred rollers changed from their original form, the practice has become less common as roller owners appreciate the historic nature of their charges. Once upon a time, a roller was seen as the lowest of the forms of steam preservation; while it is still true that their prices are not particularly high, the status of the honest working steam roller as a piece of historic machinery to enjoy has risen immeasurably. The general interest in history and heritage in the country, helped by specialist groups such as the National Traction Engine Trust, Road Locomotive Society and the Road Roller Association has meant that the place of the road roller in transport history is assured.

The Road Roller Association (RRA) was established in 1974 by a handful of roller enthusiasts, and now numbers over 1,500 members. It's not necessary to own a roller to be a member; the RRA welcomes all those with an interest in road-making in all its forms. Demonstrations are arranged at various locations of stone crushing and traditional road-making and members and others are encouraged to take part. They provide a quarterly

Over 150 steam rollers have been altered from their original form into traction engines and showman's-style engines. Increasingly this practice has reduced over the decades, but some rare machines have changed in appearance. MAN 57, a Fowler roller which worked on the Isle of Man, now looks like a showman's engine, very different from its appearance here at Stafford County Showground.

magazine called *Rolling*, full of useful historic and contemporary articles, news and letters. A considerable archive collection exists for the benefit of members. In addition, advice and assistance can be given with regard to insurance. As well as the *Rolling* magazine, the RRA also publishes a motor roller register of all known surviving motor rollers in the UK that it has been notified about and this is currently on its fourth edition. Other publications have included a reprint of Batho's paper to the IMechE, *On a Steam Road Roller*, as well as *Notes for a Successful Road Making Display* and Lyndon Shearman's life story as the last owner-operator of a road roller in the UK. It's worth saying that Lyndon was one of the founders of the RRA, the inaugural meeting of enthusiasts being held at his home in Halifax. The Association can also provide assistance with regaining registration numbers for rollers under restoration and has a wide network of contacts for resources, drawings, spares and patterns – along with a vibrant sales section.

The National Traction Engine Trust is also very much supportive of steam rollers and their heritage, as the premier body representing steam heritage on the roads of the UK and their magazine *Steaming* has many articles and images of rollers, both on the rally field and at working days. Similarly, the well-respected Road Locomotive Society considers rollers, operators and contractors and has a splendid journal. They have also published books of working day photographs and a number of reproduction makers' catalogues which are well worth seeking out as affordable alternatives to the originals.

When the first steam rallies were held in the 1950s, they were traction engine rallies, and it was only after a couple of years that rollers began to appear. Bear in mind that many

Preservation in all its facets has allowed many opportunities to recreate the past. Some have been intentional, others not. In the latter case must be this photo, taken in November 2016 at the Welland Valley Vintage Traction Club yard at Market Harborough, where a pair of Aveling rollers gives an impression of what must have been a daily occurrence in contractors' and council yards all over the country.

were still at work in commercial use, and it was not unknown for a steam roller to be driven off a job to an event, shown and driven back to work again. Some of the earliest rollers to appear didn't survive into preservation as we know it! As the 1950s moved into the 1960s, steam rollers began to join traction engines and other road-going steam vehicles on the heritage scene. The last commercially working steam roller with a council was Sussex County Council's Marshall roller with driver Allen Pronger, both retiring in 1986. Since then, steam rollers have been used commercially but by enthusiasts as one off or special jobs. Some councils still own a number of steam rollers, but as heritage pieces rather than working plant.

The steam rally began as just that, a gathering of engines and often games and a parade. As time wore on, there became more of an interest in what the machines did, how and where. The creation of the RRA saw folk look at tools, equipment and techniques, and collections began. Likewise the potential of road-making demonstrations was realised and throughout the 1980s, the RRA flew the flag for undertaking authentic recreations at rallies and events across the country. By 1988, a superb weekend was had with rollers, men and tar at the Black Country Museum in an urban setting, and although hard and dirty work, the standard had been set for others to follow. Motor rollers joined in the fun and the author recalls a busy County of Salop rally in the early 1990s where we rebuilt an estate road, seeing the process through from crushing and transporting stone to laying it and rolling it. Never have I ached so much, but it did stand a number of us in good stead for rebuilding a church car park in Aberystwyth, in which we laid 150 tons of stone and rolled it all with a former Aberystwyth Council steam roller. Since then, many events have road-making displays, whether static equipment or working. The former Tallington and Holcot rallies were particularly good active demonstrations, the latter even having its own narrow gauge railway moving material, as some sites did with civil engineering contractors. The premier annual show has to be the Great Dorset Steam Fair, where the RRA have a sales and hospitality marquee, rollers and equipment on static display and a marvellous road-building section, complete in every detail right down to the kettle boiling over an open brazier. In the north of England, Beamish Museum has held similar displays, while the Craske family in North Yorkshire show a marvellous array of tackle along with their Fowler steam roller fitted with tar pump and sprayer gear as it was when working with David Wood of Yeadon – truly a delight to behold. On a number of occasions, the RRA has published notes on road-making and carrying out a successful road-building display – written by founder Lyndon Shearman.

A steam, diesel or petrol road roller has been an accessible entry point into the preservation world for hundreds, if not thousands. Their popular appeal has endured, and although prices have risen, with care and prudence it is still just about possible for a young person or a family to buy a steam roller. Motor rollers are cheaper still and you can get a surprising amount of machine for little more than scrap value on occasion, even now. Every so often, the author will get an email or phone call advising of a derelict roller in a hedgerow, yard or field looking for a home, and it's good to report that, by and large, this has ended up with contacts being made and the rollers making their way into the hands of enthusiasts who will love, care and restore them. Rollers appear in plant sales, vintage auctions or even on eBay or Facebook; one magazine on the newsstand caters for the enthusiast, called *Classic Plant and Machinery*. It often has news or features on rollers plus a comprehensive classified adverts section; likewise for the well-established heritage magazines *Old Glory* and *Vintage Spirit*.

A small part of the historic roadmaking equipment owned and displayed by the Craske family of North Yorkshire includes their living van, tar boiler, notices and tools. Along with the Fowler roller, they show perhaps one of the finest collections of material regularly displayed anywhere in the country.

The steam roller parked up in a children's playground was once a familiar sight. This is the Aveling that used to be in Victoria Park, Leamington Spa, in April 1965. It's now fully restored and attends rallies and events in Cheshire.

Several dozen road rollers entered preservation in the 1960s and 1970s as features in children's playgrounds. With parts removed or welded up and painted in bright colours, they were popular playthings, given by councils or local contractors. At one point, the RRA published a booklet, *Parked Up Rollers*, giving the locations of these machines from Aberfeldy to Dorchester and all points between. Eddisons in particular passed on old rollers and quite often painted them in approximations of their working-day liveries, which became reds, blues, oranges and yellows as time passed. Legislation and the rise of the risk assessment saw many rollers condemned as play pieces in the 1980s and 1990s, but by that time most were recognised for the heritage items they had become. Put up for sale or sometimes given away, very few ended up as scrap – though this was the fate of some motor rollers that didn't get recognised for what they were. An Aveling DX at a school in Darlington was lost in the 1990s, ten years before the author moved to the area and enquired after it. There are only a handful of diesel rollers now in playgrounds, if

There are only two steam rollers remaining in playgrounds in the UK, Eddisons placing this one in Dorchester, a fitting location given the firm's origins in the town. It remains both as a plaything and as a reminder to the heritage of the region.

Many restored rollers have been returned to the condition in which they spent part of their working life. This motor roller perhaps bucks that trend and is displayed in its full playground colours!

any; the last the author saw was at Chesterton in Cambridge around the year 2000. Steam rollers remain in the two parks at Aberfeldy and Dorchester and look set to remain there ad infinitum. Often calls are made that they too should be released and restored, but the continued care and protection of them means that children continue to enjoy them as they have for over five decades and they also stand as reminders of another form of preservation.

It is true to say that playgrounds in parks and schools saved several dozen rollers for posterity. At least one diesel roller on the rally circuit in North Yorkshire appeared at one show in its playground colours of blue, red and yellow, but fully restored and in working order!

Did you know?

The borough of Camden buried their playground steam roller in the 1970s when it was deemed unsafe. Dug up again in the 1990s, it was restored to operation and is now cared for and has been seen at vintage shows and rallies since that time.

It's hard to believe this Aveling steam roller was once buried in the London Borough of Camden. Exhumed in the 1990s and restored by Ron and David Walker and family, it was a regular sight on the roads around Arthog in Mid-Wales in the ownership of the late David and Ritta Black.

Rollers on Display

The Continental phenomenon of putting rollers on plinths as public display items seems not to have caught on in the UK, apart from one or two locations where contractors have mounted them at yard entrances such as Swadlincote, Clee Hill and Chirk. Eye-catching adverts, they also serve to show the heritage of the contracting firms themselves, Clee Hill being one of the longer established operations. Their display of a 1940s Road Marshall is thus entirely appropriate and very welcome. There is also a rare Aveling Barford DY in the Miners' Welfare Park at Bedworth in Warwickshire, and until recently a plant hire firm in Hereford had a small Barford & Perkins mounted at their yard entrance. There are undoubtedly more, as there are rollers still waiting to be found at various locations around the country.

A number of rollers are on display in museums, from traditional static exhibits in places such as Swansea, Glasgow and Bradford to working machines at open air museums such as the East Anglian Transport Museum or Beamish. There's a huge collection at Thursford in Norfolk, where the late George Cushing laid up a working fleet and then added to their number from other sources. In recent times about a dozen rollers left the collection, but a large number remain, many in the condition they finished their working lives in. As such they make a fantastic research resource for people wanting to know the exact details for restoration projects; they also draw a comparison with the hundreds of restored rollers on the

The traditional museum display of static exhibits has in recent years given way in many places to displaying an object in context. Hampshire Museums' Milestones in Basingstoke has recreated street scenes to display their transport collection, which includes this Taskers roller, made in 1926 and the last of its make to be built.

Above: It isn't just about steam rollers. The collection at Abbey Pumping Station in Leicester includes a selection of fascinating motor rollers, including this tiny Aveling-Barford, smaller than the maker's standard GA series.

Right: For every roller on display in a museum, there are others to be found in museum stores, for there just isn't the space to show everything! This venerable Aveling & Porter roller dates from 1892 and used to be on show in steam in the old Birmingham Museum of Science & Industry. It's now in the museum collections centre and can be seen on regular open days or specialist tours.

rally scene. Other museums celebrate particular manufacturers such as the Burrell Museum in Thetford, Milestones in Basingstoke or the Long Shop Museum for Garretts in Leiston. The Museum of Lincolnshire Life displays some very rare Ruston and Robey motor rollers in the city of their construction. At the East Anglian Transport Museum, a special display exists looking at the life and practicality of road making with steam rollers entitled 'Tar, Sweat and Steam', which includes the museum's own Armstrong Whitworth steam roller and other equipment. Amberley Museum in Sussex has a fabulous sub-museum, the Museum of Roads and Road Making, supported by the Worshipful Company of Paviors and is well worth a visit, looking as it does as at a variety of eras and a large and differing collection of equipment, far beyond the simple roller and into such things as concrete roads and laying machinery, the like of which is not preserved anywhere else.

The toy road roller has been around for almost as long as the real thing. Live steam and clockwork toys were the initial ones available, made in the UK and abroad. Latterly die-cast and plastic push-along toys and models have also joined those initial offerings, the numbers and varieties produced running into hundreds, from tiny rollers in Christmas crackers to large plastic construction toys. Traditional steam rollers are still made in China as automatically reversing clockwork tin toys, while in the UK, companies such as Oxford Die-Cast and Lledo are making OO scale model Fowler and Burrell steam rollers at very affordable prices. The author's own collection runs to over 200 model and toy rollers covering all sizes, makes and materials. Perhaps the most moving model I have is one made by a blind enthusiast who could only go by the sense of touch and who therefore built what he thought a steam roller should feel like – amazing!

If one wishes to put your own specific look to a model, then a number of whitemetal or plastic kits have been made in varying scales. In OO – or 4 mm to the foot scale for the railway modeller – Aveling, Wallis and Robey tandem steam rollers are produced, as well as some motor rollers. In N – or 2 mm scale – Aveling diesel and steam rollers can be had as well as a tiny replica of a Wallis & Steevens light Advance such as the PE/D or OF/D model; the parts take some handling but a faithful model results. Going to the larger scales of O gauge (7 mm) or 1 (10 mm) the detail gets better and some superb kits exist of Aveling & Porter steam rollers in these scales and a Wallis Simplicity in the O gauge scale from Duncan Models. It goes without saying that these are also supported with a range of accessories, including tar boiler, water cart and living van.

A selection of model rollers grace the author's bookshelves. These here are a mixture of repainted Matchbox Models of Yesteryear and a couple of whitemetal kits by Springside Models.

Did you know?

The first Lesney, then later Matchbox, model was an Aveling-Barford diesel roller. Dinky also made a popular version for many years.

Thousands of the British Mamod steam rollers have been sold since their introduction in the 1960s, and at one point, the spirit fired toy was listed as 'Toy of the Year'. They have introduced the joys of live steam to many, and while I asked for one for Christmas in 1984, it was another thirty years before I finally got one! However Father Christmas did bring me a Wilesco 'Old Smoky' roller, which still occasionally sees steam for my daughter Charlotte, who has become proficient at steaming up. The German Wilesco has the edge over Mamod for realism, having a reciprocating cylinder, gears and chain steering, as opposed to the Mamod's oscillating cylinder, drive band and steering road – but both have their own charm and are great fun. If you want to go further, there are Markie live steam models, then on to model engineering kits and ready-made – though rollers are quite rare in the larger scales. It is always a pleasure to see a working road roller made by a model engineer – and I say road roller, for the designer Edgar T. Westbury created a miniature design for a working Aveling-Barford DX type complete with an operational internal combustion engine.

Model engineering extends to internal combustion rollers as well as steam, and Eleanor Wood's model DX was on show at the 2008 Road Roller Association Annual General Meeting.

1½ Inch Scale Model
of an Aveling-Barford Type "DX"
Road Roller.

To a design by Edgar. T. Westbury
and featured in Model Engineer 1938

Owned by Miss Eleanor Wood

PLEASE DO NOT TOUCH, THANK YOU

Did you know?

If you are in London and near the Institution of Mechanical Engineers on Birdcage Walk, pop in and ask to see the Cherry Hill model collection. Cherry Hill is one of the finest model engineers ever, and her skills have seen her create a number of very finely detailed working model steam rollers, from a Wallis & Steevens Advance to a model Aveling-Batho roller from 1870 and even an unusual French Gellerat steam roller, showing an interesting comparison to the English machines.

Collecting road roller-related material is another pastime if one cannot run to a full-size roller or have space for models. Photographs, postcards and books abound at events and on internet sites. Preservation-era books such as Whitehead's classic *A Century of Steam Rolling* will always be popular with its survey of builders, development of rollers, firms and stories of the men who worked with them. Also popular are Michael Lane's books on the various steam builders who made rollers, including his classics on Avelings, Fowlers, Burrells and Marshalls, while photo albums of working day steam rollers by John Crawley and others provide a link to the past. Some company histories are well worth seeking out as well, two being Aveling-Barford's *One Hundred Years for Road Rollers* and the illustrated history of Eddisons Ltd, titled *A Century of Service*. Likewise, some of the larger companies had their own house magazines – Road Rollers Limited being one – looking at the work of the business, but also the social lives and activities of the staff across the various depots in the country. A different approach with literature is manuals and textbooks on road-making from working days, and often these contain chapters on rolling, with details of how rollers were to be selected and worked. It's possible to collect manuals, catalogues and working day photos quite easily, although some of the steam catalogues can be highly priced on occasions.

Road-making lamps, tools and ephemera are popular, as are brass makers' plates, works plates and other fittings such as the Aveling rampant horse or the Marshall brass Britannia. All make great display pieces and interesting talking points if you are allowed them in domestic spaces! I have a print from an Aveling catalogue framed on the wall as a fortieth birthday card, produced by the specialist heritage printers Gone to Press and it's lovely. As the BBC might say, 'Other rollers are available,' of course...

The iconography of the road roller is long and illustrious. Perhaps because of its place in the public eye mending roads and highways, it has more of a shared experience with the populace than its ancestor and cousin the steam traction engine. Children's books have been written about rollers by such authors as Graham Greene, while a steam roller called George is a character in the Revd W. Awdry's *Railway Series*, which feature Thomas the Tank Engine. The Ladybird book *Tootles the Taxi* had a page devoted to 'Stumbles the Steam Roller', which was of course very well thumbed, and later on, in the late 1990s, the popular children's television series *Bob the Builder* features an animated motor roller called Roley. There are steam rollers featured in the *Dad's Army* television series and in the feature film *The Iron Maiden*. A motor roller is also part of a sequence in *A Fish Called Wanda* and there are no doubt others. In the annual Lord Mayor's Show in London, part of the Worshipful Company of Paviors' display includes a float pulled by a steam roller and this always reaches prime time television as it is transmitted live. Even Weston's Cider Old Rosie has as its emblem

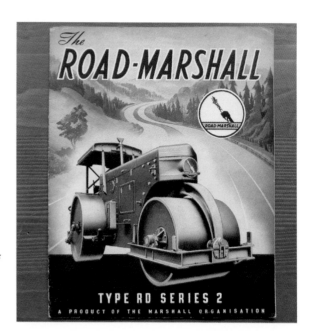

Roller-related literature can be a more affordable way of enjoying road rollers if you don't have the space or money for the real thing or a large model. This and other items were picked up off eBay for a few pounds!

Polite Motorist (after the accident). "I DO TRUST I HAVEN'T DAMAGED YOUR CHASSIS!"

In popular culture, the road roller has always been seen as an object of fun and satire. This cartoon from *Punch* magazine from 1913 shows how roller humour has lasted over a century.

an Aveling steam roller, owned by the company and used in publicity! We've already noted of course the universal use of the term 'steam roller' in the English language, whether it is describing the piece of equipment parked up in the middle of the M1 as we travel south, or the latest attempt of the government of the time to pass a piece of legislation without opposition.

If you are interested in family or local history, road rollers unlock stories of companies, individuals, councils, towns and engineers. One photo of a roller with a few notes can turn into a research project and introduce you to a whole set of new people. Looking at old photos and working out where they are shows how much the world has changed – or indeed how little on occasion. A number of roller owners have taken researching their machines to a whole new and deeper level, on occasions going back to locations and recreating scenes from the past in more recent years. The growth of the internet has seen many record offices and archives creating websites and making a lot more images accessible. A simple search for 'steam roller' on one such as Windows on Warwickshire will provide a good number of pictures and an absorbing evening or two.

On the high street, the roller enthusiast is catered for by the monthly magazines *Old Glory* and *Vintage Spirit*, both of which regularly carry news and articles on rollers. The editors of both are also roller enthusiasts who strongly support the Road Roller Association. In the world of the internet, the RRA has a website and a very active Facebook page, which showcases steam and motor rollers, historic and contemporary pictures, plus news and sales of rollers. A number of other pages exist looking at particular makers or even types of engine – there is one for Aveling E type steam rollers for example!

The road roller occupies a unique place in British history and to a degree internationally. While the steam traction engine might be considered mainly an agricultural machine, the road roller spreads across the land, spanning town and country, wherever roads needed making or repairing. Small children were inspired to become engineers because they saw the roller at work in their formative years and the steam roller has become a comforting figure of transport heritage, loved by many. Long may it continue!

The history of a road roller can lead into further research into family and local history. These simple notes from Bishop Auckland resident Graham Redfearn have led into a feature in the local newspaper and shared memories and information as a result.

A further collectors' piece can be old manuals and parts lists – which can be of great value if you are running or restoring an old roller too. This Aveling parts diagram dates back to 1914.

To end the book, we conclude with three images to show how far the preservation of the road roller has come. This first photo was taken in April 2016 at Beamish Museum's Great North Steam Fair. Brian Knight's Ruston, Proctor steam roller rests in the colliery yard in a scene that could easily have been from a hundred years earlier.

Above: In a layby near Tywyn, Gwynedd, in May 2006, Ian Cooper's Aveling steam roller waits for its transport home after the Tom Rolt Vintage Rally. Keeping company with a Foden diesel lorry, Ian's roller worked for Staffordshire County Council and was dry stored from the 1960s until pretty much when Ian bought it in 2006. Presented as a working engine, it represents very well the latter years of commercial steam rolling.

Below: The sun sets in County Durham on Michael Davison's Armstrong Whitworth steam roller *Albert*, not long after he returned it to the North East where it began its working life in the 1920s.